Drawing Is Basic
Drawing and Writing to Learn

PRE-KINDERGARTEN

Drawing is a basic way of seeing and expressing. Every child can draw, but too many children are daunted by the fear that what they draw will not look "right." It is your joyous opportunity to encourage each of your students to draw and write with comfort and confidence.

Jean Morman Unsworth

DALE SEYMOUR PUBLICATIONS®

Parsippany, New Jersey

Editorial Manager: Carolyn Coyle
Senior Editor: Mary Ellen Gilbert
Production/Manufacturing Director: Janet Yearian
Production/Manufacturing Manager: Karen Edmonds
Production/Manufacturing Coordinator: Lorraine Allen
Art Director: Jim O'Shea
Text and Cover Design: Robert Dobaczewski

Credits

Chagall, Marc, 1887–1985, *House in Pestowatik,* p. 76, 1922, etching. Courtesy of R. S. Johnson International Gallery, Chicago, IL.

Cassatt, Mary, 1844–1926, *Mother and Child,* p. 53, color aquatint. Courtesy of R. S. Johnson International Gallery, Chicago, IL.

Corinth, Lovis, 1858–1925, *The Cow,* p. 56. Etching and drypoint. Courtesy of R. S. Johnson International Gallery, Chicago, IL.

Unsworth, Jean Morman, *Trees,* p. 41, pencil drawing; *Hot Air Balloons,* p. 43, photograph; *Bird High Rise,* work of Dan Yarborough, p. 74, photograph; *Sandhill Crane,* p. 62, ink drawing; *Flying Insects,* p. 69, brush drawing; *Williamsburg House,* p. 79, photograph.

Unsworth, Jean and Tim's Collection: Mola, *Monkey,* p. 57; Mola, *Bird,* p. 64; *Etruscan horse* (copy), p. 55, bronze; *Inuit Bird,* p. 63, soapstone.

Slinky® is a registered trademark of James Industries, Inc. Use of this trademark implies no relationship, sponsorship, endorsement, sale or promotion on the part of Dale Seymour Publications® Inc.

Dale Seymour Publications
An imprint of Pearson Learning
299 Jefferson Road, P.O. Box 480
Parsippany, New Jersey 07054-0480
www.pearsonlearning.com
1-800-321-3106

Dale Seymour Publications® is a registered trademark of Dale Seymour Publications, Inc.

ISBN 0-7690-2493-9

1 2 3 4 5 6 7 8 9 10-ML-04 03 02 01 00

This Book Is Printed
On Recycled Paper

This book is written with the hope that all who read it will catch the confidence and the clear eyes of a child and, whatever their age, risk the pleasure of really seeing.

Some years ago, on a flight to Vancouver, I sat with two little girls who were on their way home from a visit with their grandparents in Chicago. I got them drawing—what else? When I asked them to draw a picture of me, the four-year-old said, "I can't." I said, "Of course you can. Just look at me." This is my portrait by her. I lost her name, but I treasure the portrait.

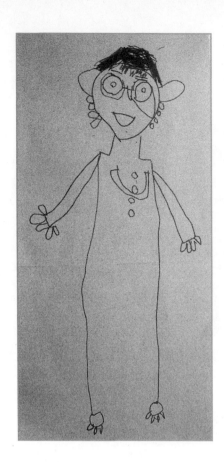

Jean Morman Unsworth

Thanks to the teachers who piloted the lessons in *Drawing Is Basic* and who sent in their students' drawings.

Lin Ferrell
Visual Arts Instructional Specialist
Chesterfield County Public Schools
Richmond, Virginia, and the
art teachers of Chesterfield County

Teri Power, art specialist
School District of
New Richmond, Wisconsin

Eva Dubowski, art teacher
Infant of Prague School
Flossmoor, Illinois

Andrea Rowe, classroom teacher
St. Damian School
Oak Forest, Illinois

Catherine Kestler, art teacher,
and classroom teachers of
Sacred Heart Academy
Chicago, Illinois

Barbara Perez, art teacher
St. Athanasius School
Evanston, Illinois

Dorothy Johnson, art supervisor
Volusia County Schools
Florida

Additional thanks to the classroom teachers in the following Chicago, Illinois, schools: St. Matthias School, Children of Peace School, and St. Gertrude School.

A special thank you to all the young artists who performed the drawing exercises in this book and whose drawings add a unique charm to *Drawing Is Basic*.

Katie Meyers

Cameron Thrift

Alexander Sanchez

Christian Aquino

Jack Sommer

Michelle Mitchell

Carlos Pinto

Alexander Sanchez

Nick Orosz

Kirsten Schafer

Asia Szczepaniak

Jose Bautista

Raphaella Tran

Camille Hoang

Mark Deufel

Jennifer Stanley

Jessica Mitchell

Eddie Bindewald

Steven Herrera

Renee Orivida

Alexa Imaoka

Kristina Speck

Meggan Solomine

Liliana Fernandez

Christopher Nelson

Christopher Pinto

Caroline Donnelly

Margaret Isaacson

Ellie O'Connor

Justice Harvieux

Andrew Rowe

Dan Rowe

Rebecca Born

Ian Bisinger

Emily Zeller

Madison Radway

Reyna Lute

Christian Aquino

Stephen

Eddie

Margaret

Contents

1. Warm-up Exercises

p.21

2. Following Directions

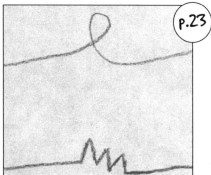

p.23

3. Connecting to All of Your Senses

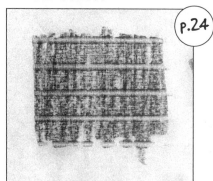

p.24

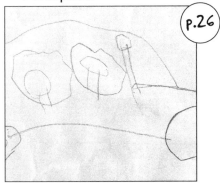
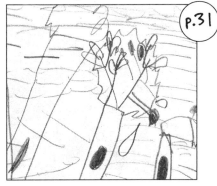

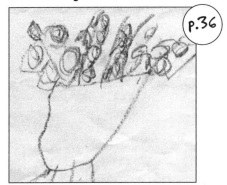

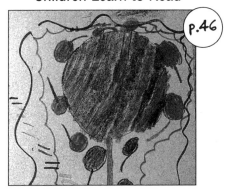

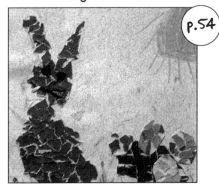

16. Drawing Fish

p.65

17. Drawing Insects

p.68

18. Drawing Buildings

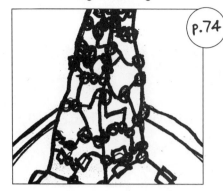

p.74

19. Drawing from Imagination

p.82

20. Encouraging Drawing at Home

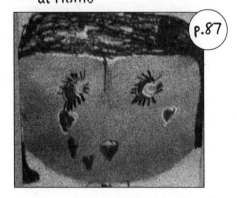

p.87

A Message to the Classroom Teacher

IT IS WITHIN THE POWER OF EVERY PERSON TO DRAW.

The natural condition of the human organism is joy. Ecstasy is not opposed to reason and order. Much of the life of the child is learning, making connections. It is momentous, joyous. It must not be quelled.

—George Leonard, *Education and Ecstasy*

Drawing is an essential means of expression, just as important as writing and oral expression in the daily work of learning. Drawing is a complementary mode of learning. It helps complete writing and verbal communication. At pre-kindergarten and kindergarten levels, drawing can be children's chief mode of expression. You, as a classroom teacher, CAN teach it. NEVER DRAW FOR CHILDREN. Just get them to LOOK and to draw with their eyes. You can help them to see details and to understand proportions, but the drawing is theirs.

Here are some important points to keep in mind about drawing.

❖ Drawing is as personal as handwriting. We all learn to shape the cursive letters the same way. Yet, we each develop a unique style of handwriting that is our identification. Our drawing style must be equally personal. Don't attempt to teach children what something should look like; rather, teach how to look. Children will see uniquely according to their levels of maturity and keenness of perception.

❖ For young children, exercises in all the sensory approaches to perception are important—sight, touch, hearing, smell, taste. When you teach perception, you are at the same time teaching reading. Reading begins with following a line of letters and looking carefully. **Perceptual** drawing helps develop that skill in a child.

❖ When children (or adults) draw by letting their eyes direct their hands, their concentration is beautiful. Try taking a drawing break when your students are restless. It calms and centers them. They will go back to their other lessons relaxed and ready.

❖ Some structured coloring is good for developing motor skills. But too much coloring of outlined images can undermine children's sense of confidence in their own drawings. Just ask them to draw five apples instead of coloring them in a book.

❖ Training children's eyes to really see is our first task as teachers. You, as a classroom teacher, should be a part of this visual learning. In an interdisciplinary learning climate, every subject should be approached both literally and expressively. A once-a-week art lesson by the art specialist cannot begin to reach these dimensions. When you help children to develop basic drawing skills, you will enable the art specialist to move in leaps rather than slow steps.

Goals of Teaching Drawing

The real point about art education is that we must create whole human beings, people who are alive to their fingertips; people who are in a responsible attitude to sensation, to every organized form, to every meaning of the world about them. To open the closed eye is the first lesson of art in our time; the second is to open the inner eye, the eye of vision and dream.

—Lewis Mumford

❖ To develop in each child the skill and confidence to draw with his or her eyes in order to use drawing as a complementary and essential mode of learning all subjects.

❖ To stimulate visual thinking as a natural mode of thinking for every child.

❖ To teach children the "language of art"—how to look for lines, shapes, spaces, textures, and colors all around them.

Every child is an artist. The problem is how to remain an artist once he grows up.

—Pablo Picasso

❖ To nurture children's sensory perception through all the senses as children spend time touching, looking, listening, smelling, tasting, and describing their perceptions—thus developing language skills.

❖ To spur the imaginations of children, encouraging them to create, invent, connect, experiment with, and enjoy their own ideas.

❖ To nurture in children the ability to express their drawing and their perception in words. At the pre-kindergarten level, encourage children to describe their drawings, or tell the story they are drawing. You may want to label drawings and display them to begin a reading vocabulary.

❖ To allow yourself the joy of drawing, thus building your own confidence and your own vision.

Challenges You May Encounter

Most children at this age love to draw and draw fearlessly, but you may encounter some of the following problems.

❖ **What if he or she won't draw or even start to draw?**
Years ago I was working with a group of four-year-olds in Georgia. One little boy would not put a mark on the paper. We were working on 18" × 24" sheets with long-handled brushes and tempera. I asked him if he could make a circle. Finally, he did—a tiny one in the lower left corner of the paper. "Beautiful!" I said. "Can you make another one?" He did—another tiny one next to the first. With gentle encouragement, he made a larger circle, moving always toward the center of the paper. Finally, he drew large circles all over the paper. It was like watching a butterfly emerge from a cocoon.

Why was he hesitant? Perhaps he had never had art materials. Perhaps he wasn't encouraged to try drawing at home. Whatever the reason, it is the teacher's privilege to lead such children to confidence and joy.

❖ **What about the child who draws quickly and carelessly?**
Use drawing time to walk around and spot children who need guidance. Quiet concentration and observation need to be cultivated in today's fast-paced world and climate of passive entertainment. "Doing it yourself" needs nurturing in many children. Set the tone before giving

the assignment. Prepare sketchbook or other materials and tools. Model looking carefully at the object, figure model, or view to be drawn. Encourage "crawling along every edge as if your eye is a bug."

❖ **What about the child who has difficulty seeing details?**
This may be a sign of a perceptual handicap such as dyslexia or other eye-hand–related dysfunctions. Spend time with this child. Run your finger along the edge to be drawn. Then have the child do it. The better the child can discipline his or her eyes to follow an edge, the better the child will read. Display many different types of objects in your classroom. Encourage children to pick them up, examine them, and feel them. Have nature photographs and videos available. Create a climate of learning.

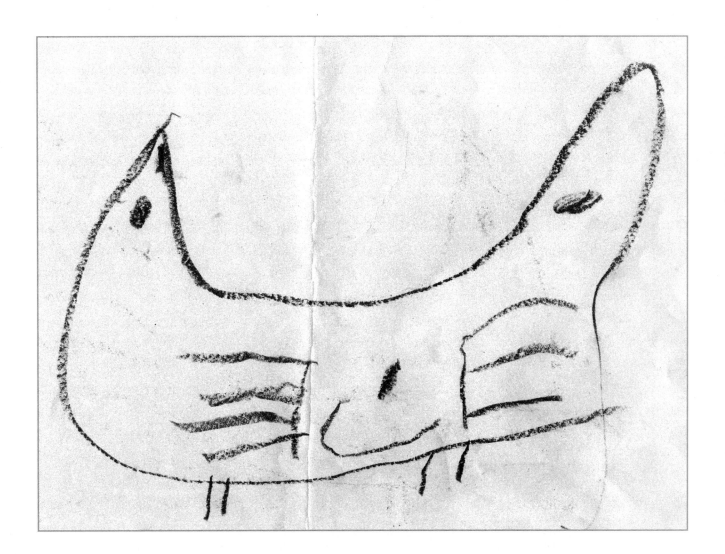

Listening to Children. The following story illustrates our need to allow much time for drawing what is on children's minds and in their hearts and to listen to what children are saying.

Harry Chapin, the folk singer, sang a song about a little boy who goes to school and starts painting flowers in many beautiful colors. The teacher says, "What are you doing, young man?" "I'm painting flowers," he says. The teacher replies, "This is not the time for art and, besides, flowers are red, green leaves are green. There's no need to see flowers any other way than the way they always have been seen." The little boy answers, "There are so many colors in the rainbow, so many colors in the rising sun, and I see every one." The teacher says, "You're sassy. Go to the corner." Finally, he gets lonesome and comes out and says, "Flowers are red, green leaves are green. There's no need to see flowers any other way than the way they always have been seen." Then, his family moves away, and he goes to a different school. The teacher says, "Use all of your colors." But he paints red flowers and green leaves. She asks why. He says, "Flowers are red, green leaves are green. There's no need to see flowers any other way than the way they always have been seen."

Drawing Is Basic

The goal of *Drawing Is Basic* is to make children comfortable with drawing objects and figures.

Set a time for drawing. Take frequent "drawing breaks." Set the stage with a minute of quiet looking at the thing children are going to draw. Talk about it, feel it, describe it. Ask children to draw in the air often. You will find that when they draw they become intensely quiet and involved. It frees them from the "response" mode and allows them to "express." Establish that kind of quiet as the way to draw. It will be a habit that will carry on through their school years.

Choose a lesson from any one of the skill sections. Each of the skills presented in the following pages needs much repetition, so vary the lessons to avoid overemphasis on any one. The lessons are offered as ideas, not material to be "covered." Choose what your students are ready to do. Relate lessons to your curriculum themes of the day.

Suggested Weekly Plans

Do the following exercises several times a day.

Week 1: Warm-up exercises—Do these periodically through the school year, often just as a one-minute exercise before the drawing lesson.

Week 2: Following directions

Week 3: Connecting to the senses

Week 4: Drawing objects, beginning perceptual drawing

Week 5: Drawing shoes

Your students' interests and skill development will direct your choices. Treat these exercises as a "drill" in perception. The carryover into reading is direct. Children are training their eyes to follow a line and look carefully at details.

Continue taking drawing breaks with your students every day, moving on to figure drawing, drawing animals, and so on. These skills need much repetition through the year.

Using the I Am an Artist Sketchbook

The children's sketchbooks have a dual purpose.

1. These sketchbooks provide the drawing paper for most of your lessons. However, for some lessons you may want to have children draw on practice paper a few times before using the sketchbook. (For cutting lessons, you will want to provide other paper such as colored construction paper.)

2. The sketchbooks also will help you keep a record of children's development. Date each page as children complete them. Periodically, spend time with your students looking back on their earlier work and using the critiquing techniques beginning on page 18 to assess children's work.

Never have children compare their work. Growth should be measured on the child's own work only.

3. Encourage children to keep their sketchbooks so that they can compare the work they do each year. These sketchbooks may be treasured when children grow up.

Prepare Sketchbook Covers.
When you think children are ready, distribute 4 1/4" × 5 1/2" sheets of paper (8 1/2" × 11" sheets cut in fourths), and have them draw self-portraits. Then, glue their drawings in the rectangle on the cover of their sketchbooks. You might have children draw monthly self-portraits to be given to parents at the end of the year.

Consider keeping children's self-portraits as a time capsule for your school year. Have each child draw his or her self-portrait. Then measure each child, weigh him or her, and record this information with the child's self-portrait. Keep them in a box until the end of the school year. At that time, have children draw another self-portrait, and again record their heights and weights. Open the box and compare the children's growth in measurements and skills.

At the beginning of the year, you might ask your students to draw small self-portraits of just their faces. Arrange children's self-portraits on the door of your classroom as a way of making the room their own.

Preparing for the Lessons

The greater the awareness of all the senses, the greater will be the opportunity for learning.

—Viktor Lowenfeld and Lambert W. Brittain

❖ Have boxes of artificial flowers, small toys, seashells, and so on, on hand. Children can contribute to these collections. Tools are simple—crayons, pencils, markers, and so on—and should be readily available.

❖ Direct children to take out their sketchbooks or distribute other paper. Select the drawing tool you wish them to use, or allow them to select their own tools.

❖ Start with the warm-up exercises to develop children's motor control. Move on when you see that they are ready. Challenge them. One kindergarten teacher says to her students, "I was going to have you do something today, but I think it's too hard." They, of course, say, "We can do it." And they do.

❖ Introduce the lesson briefly and begin drawing. Observe children who are having trouble, and help them to look carefully at their subject. Do not draw for them.

❖ Perceptual drawing is an essential way of learning. When you draw with your eyes, you see details and remember them. Direct children to let their eyes crawl like a bug along each edge, moving from one to another. Tell them to let their hands follow the path of their eyes, noting every line and detail.

❖ Spend time with children looking at objects, feeling them, running a finger along the edges, and describing their details. Artificial flowers are a good place to start. Count the petals, feel the stems and leaves. Look at toy cars. Name all the parts.

❖ Follow each drawing break with time for children to tell about their drawings.

❖ Do each of these exercises many times. Each experience of intense looking will sharpen children's perception and improve their drawings.

Tools and Materials

Drawing Tools

Crayons and markers as well as paintbrushes and tempera are your children's best drawing tools. Learning about colors is an essential element of the drawing experience for preschoolers. Spend time allowing them to draw lines that are

ANGULAR THIN
Flowing scribbly
BOLD Graceful
THICK

and many other kinds of line. Choose thick or thin tools to make each kind of line.

Drawing Materials

The *I Am an Artist* sketchbooks are intended to provide a record of children's development in drawing skills. Use them after children have been drawing a specific lesson on ordinary paper several times. Date each drawing after it is completed. This book will be a log of the childrens' growth and maturation and a means of assessment for both the child and teacher.

For cutting activities, construction paper, scissors, and glue will be needed. Kraft and other decorative papers can be an interesting addition to your supplies. For larger drawings, collect financial pages from the newspapers, or cut mural/kraft paper.

Classroom Resources

A classroom that is visually exciting is a stimulus to looking, learning, and expressing. There are many resources, both for purchase and free, that can add visual energy to your classroom. Display a variety of objects in your classroom and encourage children to pick them up, examine them, and feel them. Here are some ideas for creating a climate of learning in your classroom.

❖ A place for found objects, such as stones, small branches, a wheel from a broken toy, and other things that children like to keep in their pockets, is a source of ideas for drawing. Place these in a box or on a small table.

❖ Make nature photographs, videos, and math manipulatives available. Tapes of educational television programs will provide rich resources. Pause videos to allow children to look carefully at birds, animals, flowers, and so on. Study shapes, color, and patterns on fish, zebras, and other forms.

❖ Have a teddy bear day, a doll day, or a toy car day. Encourage children to look, feel, and notice details of things.

❖ Create a texture board or box. Encourage children to bring in pieces of cloth, paper, or other textured materials. Develop vocabulary by describing the textures.

❖ Ask nature museums to lend birds, boxes of butterflies, and other natural objects for your classroom.

❖ Visit zoos, museums, and other exhibits with children to stimulate interest in recording what they see. Encourage children to use their sketchbooks on these visits.

❖ Encourage children to take their sketchbooks on family trips and draw the things they see.

❖ Hold "what I saw on the way to school" sessions to encourage looking.

❖ Invite children to bring family or ethnic costumes to class and pose in them for a drawing session.

How do we learn? Look at the ordinary as if you have never seen it before. It takes courage, the openness of a child, and the sense of discovery. Push your imagination to its limits and it will dance.

Critiquing Techniques

Children of this age are not ready to look critically at their work. Praise is important. Recognize the uniqueness of each child's work. Hold up their drawings of animals, for example, and talk about the many ways we can see and show animals. Each drawing is special and different. Too much attention to the talented child may convince other children that they cannot draw. Praise, but do not single out those children. Display children's drawings and encourage comments on how well they show objects and details.

The Elements of Art

The elements of art—**line, shape, texture, color,** and **space**—are like parts of speech in language. They are what you use as you draw, and each element has expressive power.

❖ Line. Talk about line and ask a child to come up and trace the lines of a drawing with a finger. Just drawing lines directed by your descriptive words is a very good exercise.

❖ Shape. Look for shape, or the outline of an object. Ask children to describe the shape—round, square, fat, wiggly, and so on. Does it look like the object that was drawn? Allow children to spend time feeling the shape as well as describing it in words.

❖ Texture. Spend time feeling many textures with children. Ask for words to describe texture—soft, rough, smooth, hairy, fuzzy, and so on. Create a bulletin board display of textures from actual swatches of fabric and other materials. Have children come up to the board and, without looking, touch and describe one of the textures. Look for drawings that show texture.

❖ Color. Color is so important for the preschool child. Have children create color boxes by bringing objects or photographs of things and sorting them according to color. Draw red objects, blue objects, and so on. Mix primary colors of paint—red, yellow, blue—and discover green, orange, and purple with your children. Invent stories about a color.

❖ Space. Space as an element of art will not enter preschool children's thinking. But you can give them space problems such as drawing an object contained in a box, or drawing all the objects in their room at home.

The Principles of Art

The principles of art are the "rules" for organizing elements in artwork.

Rhythm. Ask your students to tap out rhythms on their desks, such as A, AA, A, AA. **Rhythm** is a basic principle of organizing a **composition**. It is a pattern that is created by repetition. Have children repeat rows of design, repeat colors, and so on.

Balance and Proportion. These principles of art create a pleasing order of size and arrangement of forms in a composition. Teach **symmetry—bilateral** and **radial,** as a way for children to understand these principles.

Assessment

The drawings children create during drawing breaks should not be given a grade. Help children to assess their own progress rather than their skills. Keep and date drawings, especially those in their sketchbooks, as a means of both teacher and individual assessment. Make assessment a positive experience. Ask children to compare current drawings to those done weeks before, and find ways in which they are improving. Duplicate the chart on page 94 for each child. A sample is shown below. Go over each point with your students and ask them to mark the box if they think they are improving.

Name _____

School Months

	1	2	3	4	5	6	7	8	9
uses details									
carefully colors shapes									
completes drawings									
cuts neatly									
glues neatly									
shows craftsmanship									
uses descriptions									

Additional Comments:

_____

_____

_____

_____

_____

_____

Drawing Is Basic

Drawing Exercises

All of the following drawing exercises are written as you would present them to your students. Directions and suggestions for you, the teacher, are in italic type. The ✏ icon indicates teacher dialogue.

I. Warm-up Exercises

To develop children's motor control, do many exercises in drawing lines.

✏ *(Show a Slinky®. Stretch it out and see the continuous curving line.)* Show the movement of the Slinky® in the air by moving your hand. Now, draw a Slinky® on your paper. Keep your circle going around and around. Tell about other things that keep going around and around.

✏ Draw lines that look funny, tall, wiggly, and happy. Bring your paper to the front of the class, and tell about your lines.

✏ *(Model drawing a thick line with the side of a crayon.)* Draw lines that are straight, curved, or thick. Choose a tool that will make a thick line. Draw lines that are thin, long, or short.

✏ Draw circles all over your paper. Now make them into faces. Tell about your people. Are they happy?

✏ *(Take a line walk around the room or outside.)* Look for different kinds of lines. *(Make a list of the lines children saw.)* Draw some of the lines we saw.

✏ *(Take a color walk.)* Find all the reds you can see; then all the yellows, and so on. Can you find many kinds of red? Of yellow? Of blue? Find dark ones and light ones. Tell about the colors you find.

✏ *(Take a shape walk.)* **Find square shapes, long shapes, wide shapes, and tall shapes. Find and name many kinds of shapes.**

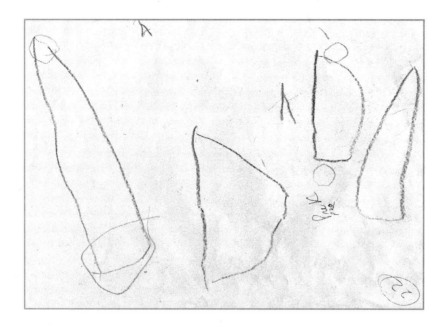

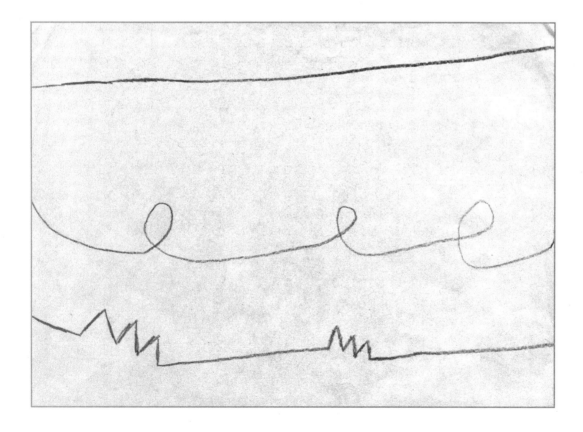

2. Following Directions

- Use your crayons. Draw three lines from the left side of your paper to the right side. Now draw three lines from the top of your paper to the bottom. Now, use different colors of crayons and draw circles in each section. Talk about why you chose your colors.

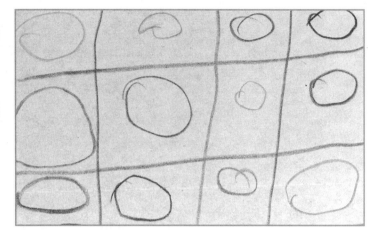

- Draw lines that go up, down, and across your paper.

- Draw five dots on your paper. Now, draw lines to connect the dots. Make your drawing into something funny. Tell about it.

- Draw a large box. Now draw a smaller box. Draw another box near the smaller box. Now draw things inside your boxes. Tell the class about your drawings.

- Draw a circle at the top of your paper. Now draw a square at the bottom of your paper. Draw lines in the middle of your paper to connect the circle and square. What could your drawing be? Could it be a hot air balloon? Tell about what you drew.

- Use a large marker or the side of a piece of crayon. Draw a wide line. Now draw a narrow line. What tool will you use? Fill your paper with wide and narrow lines. Use three colors to make a design. Tell about why you chose your colors.

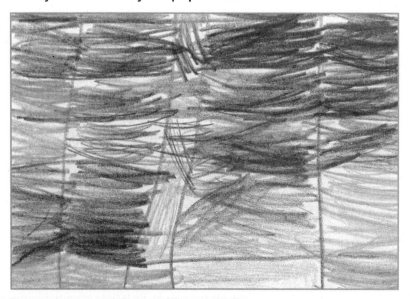

- Draw a line from the top of your paper to the bottom. Repeat the line five more times. Now draw five lines from the right side of your paper to the left side. Color each little square that you have made.

3. Connecting to All of Your Senses

- Describe a picture or an object that you have in your desk. Ask other children to guess what it is.

- *(Take a texture walk.)* Feel as many surfaces and objects as you can. Think of words to describe how they feel—fuzzy, rough, smooth, hard, and so on.

- Bring textured things to school to put on our bulletin board. Look for sandpaper, cardboard, pieces of fabric, tree bark, and rug samples. *(Play a blindfold game.)* Touch the bulletin board, and try to name the texture you touch.

Take a blind walk. Blindfold one child and, as you walk around the room, ask the child to describe what is touched. Elicit good descriptive words. If the child cannot identify the object, ask others to give hints.

- *(Hold up a toy, such as a stuffed animal or a truck, and allow time for children to describe what they see in detail. Then put it away.)* Use your memory. Draw a picture of what you have been describing.

- *(Play a musical selection.)* Listen to the music. Move your arms and hands to go with the music. Now draw lines that look like the music. Is the music bouncy? Smooth? Quick? Is it like a march?

- *(Give each child a cookie.)* Describe your cookie. Tell about its shape, color, and the way it looks. Smell it. Tell about the smell. Take a bite and describe how it tastes. Eat your cookie. Now draw a large picture of it.

Make a texture box. Ask children to bring pieces of fabric, paper, or small objects (plastic bottle caps, tassels, brushes, and so on) to school. Glue the objects on the inside of a cardboard box. Cut a circle in one side just large enough for a hand to reach in. Have children reach in, feel something, and tell what they think it is. Make sure there are no sharp edges in the box.

✐ Find textured surfaces in the classroom or outside. Lay your paper on the surface, and rub it with a crayon to make a pattern. Do many sheets of rubbings. *(Cut out shapes from children's rubbings and put them all together into a class design.)*

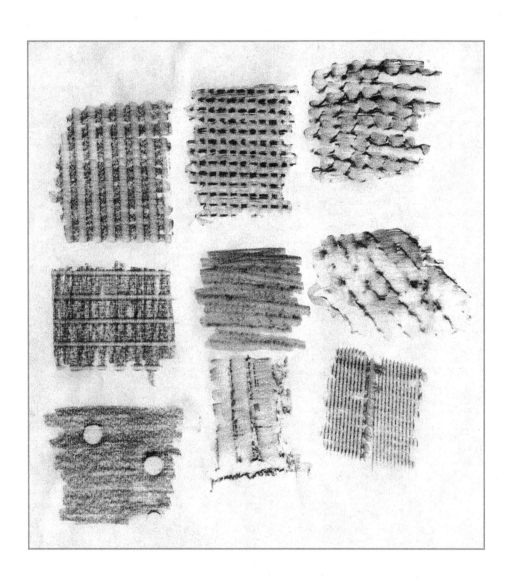

4. Exercises in Perception

These exercises are designed to get children to look carefully and recall details of familiar things. Spend time looking and talking about objects before children draw them.

✏ *(Show a toy truck.)* **Look at this toy truck. Find circles in the truck. Find long lines. Come up and run your finger along these lines. Find doors and windows. What else do you see? Now draw a toy truck. Tell about your drawing.**

This drawing is by a pre-kindergarten child who looked at a toy truck.

Christian Aquino

✏ Draw the long part and the tip of each of your crayons. Use a different color to draw each crayon.

✏ How many wheels does a wagon have? What shape is a wagon? Can you sit in it? What can you carry in a wagon? Draw your wagon. Tell a story about it.

Have children draw shoes on paper several times before drawing in their sketchbooks. Save all the drawings so they can be a means of comparing and assessing both for you and your students.

✏ Take off one shoe. Turn it around and look at each side of it. Does it look different from each side? Run your finger along your shoe. Put your shoe on your desk and your paper flat in front of it. Start drawing at the top back of the shoe. Let your eyes move along the edge toward the front. Draw your shoe as large as you can on your paper. As your eyes move along, let your hand and tool follow the way it moves. Draw everything you see on your shoe—lines for the sole, laces, and so on. Tell about the parts of the shoe that you saw and drew. Talk about why shoes are important to you.

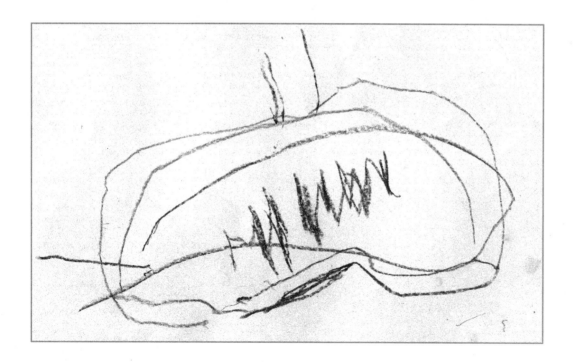

✏️ Look at all the parts of a toy telephone. Draw the telephone.

These drawings of a toy telephone were done by pre-kindergarten children. One drew the whole shape. Another drew an airplane from the hand piece. He also looked at the hand piece and drew three bats.

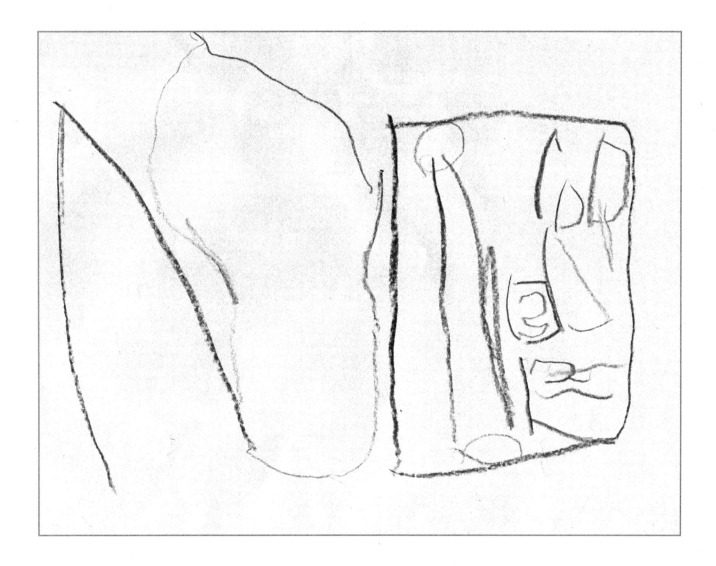

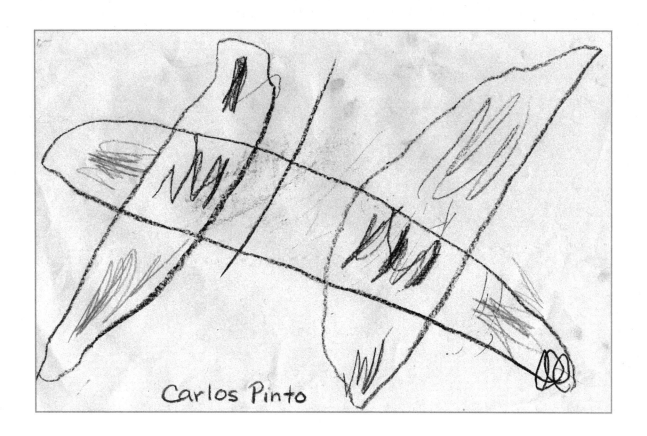

Carlos Pinto

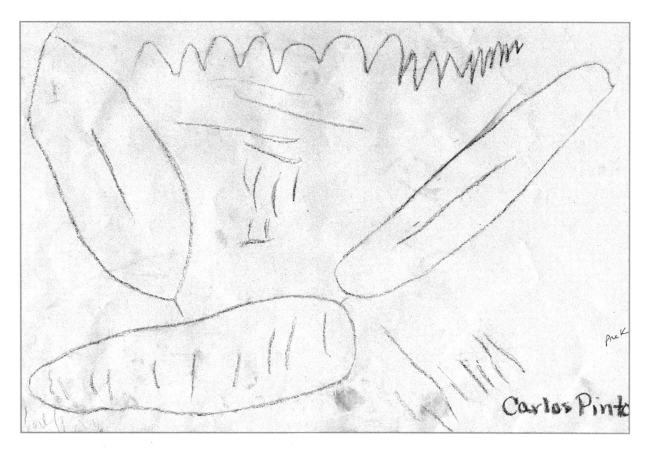

Carlos Pinto

Drop a stone in a shallow pan of water and watch the ripples. Talk about the circular pattern and how the ripples grow larger.

✏ Draw the tiny stone in the center of your paper. Draw the ripples as they grow larger and larger.

✏ *(Show children an example of a **repeat pattern**.)* Find repeat patterns—in clothes, in window blinds, and in other places in the classroom. Start at the top of your paper and draw a line across the paper. Now draw a small zigzag line under that line. Repeat lines all over your paper. Choose a different color crayon for each line. Make each line different.

5. Drawing the Weather

✏ Draw a rainy day. How does the rain look? What color is the sky on a rainy day? Tell the story of your drawing. *(These are five-year-olds' drawings of rain and clouds.)*

✏ Draw many zigzag lines across your paper. Imagine that it is a lightning storm. Tell a story about it.

Teach the colors of the rainbow: red, orange, yellow, green, blue, and purple. Tell children that the outside of the rainbow is red. For a complete learning experience, bring a prism to class and show a light spectrum with it.

- ✏ Draw a rainbow. *(Direct the sequence of colors.)* When do you usually see a rainbow? Tell about rainbows you have seen.

- ✏ Draw a picture of what it looks like in the winter. Draw a snowman. Where else will you show snow? Make up a song about your snowman.

- ✏ *(Distribute sheets of light blue construction paper.)* When you look at clouds, do you ever see other shapes in them? Use a white crayon and draw clouds. Make them puffy. Make them look like something. Tell about your drawing.

- ✏ How do things look when the wind is blowing? Draw a windstorm. Draw some leaves flying around. Are the trees bent? Tell about a time when you were out in a storm.

- ✏ Pretend you are in the rain with an umbrella. Is the wind blowing? Does your umbrella turn inside out? Draw a picture of yourself in the rain. Tell a story about it.

- ✏ *(The sun helps plants and flowers grow, warms us, melts the snow, and so on.)* Draw a picture of the sun in the sky. Now draw what the sun does for us. Tell about your drawing.

6. Drawing Food

✏ *(Present the three basic needs of food, shelter, and clothing and discuss them.)* Draw food, a place to live, and clothing for an imaginary person.

✏ Draw two apples, three oranges, and four bananas. Draw large and color each drawing. *(Use the drawings to practice counting. Have three or four children hold up their drawings as the class counts the number of objects in each.)*

✏ *(Teach the four basic food groups—fruits and vegetables, grains, dairy, and meats and fish.)* Draw your favorite food in each group. *(Show all of the drawings. Talk about how each food tastes and its nutritional value. Arrange the drawings in a food pyramid on a bulletin board.)*

For the following exercise, you might have children draw a circle with lines, dividing it into six sections, or distribute a paper on which the sectioned circle is drawn. If possible, display a color wheel.

✏ Name a food for each of these colors: red, orange, yellow, green, blue, and purple. In each section of your wheel, draw a food that is one of these colors.

✏ *(Distribute white paper plates.)* Draw your favorite meal. Tell about what you like to eat.

Draw 9" circles on 9" × 12" manila drawing paper. Cut out a circle for each child, or have children cut out their own circles using blunt scissors.

✏ Make the circle into a pizza with your favorite toppings. Use colors for cheese, pepperoni, peppers, and other things. *(Display the pizzas in the room.)* Tell a story about your family eating a pizza.

✏ Draw a large drinking glass on your sketchbook page. Pretend that you fill it with soda pop. Draw tiny bubbles in it. Talk about your favorite drink.

7. Drawing Flowers

Distribute a variety of artificial flowers. Teach the parts of a flower as a science lesson, and have children touch the flower parts.

✏ Draw a vase of flowers. Look at each flower to see its design. Count the petals. Look at the shape of the leaves. Use many colors. *(Make up a class poem about the vase of flowers.)*

✏ Draw four circles. Add petals, stems, and leaves to make four beautiful flowers. Can you name some kinds of flowers that have circles in the middle and petals around them?

✏ Draw a garden filled with flowers. Draw a bee flying over your flowers. Tell about how bees make honey.

✏ *(In spring, have children find and draw dandelions.)* Draw the dandelions' bright yellow petals.

(A few days later, find dandelions that have gone to seed.) Draw the white puffball shapes and the tiny seeds flying off. Look carefully at the jagged shape of dandelion leaves. Draw them, too. Tell a story about your dandelions.

✏ *(If possible, drip wax from a lighted candle all over sheets of paper.)* Pretend these drops of wax are the centers of a whole garden of flowers. Draw petals, stems, and leaves around each drop of wax.

Here is a child's example.

35

8. Drawing Trees

*Organic **branching** is the growth pattern found in many forms in nature. Start with a bulletin board of branching forms. Display pictures or diagrams of everything from a small twig to the pattern of blood vessels in the body. Explain to children how lightning branches, cracks in the sidewalk branch, and rivers branch. Each species of tree has a unique branching pattern, too.*

Have children take pencils or crayons and sketchbooks outside on a nice day. Walk around and find different trees. Focus on one tree and look at the way the branches bend. Notice the different shapes of leaves, and feel the bark.

- Start at the base and "climb up the trunk with your eyes." Follow the line out to a branch. See it connect to a smaller branch. Keep your eyes on the tree. Draw the leaves on the tree the way that you see them.

This is a five-year-old's drawing of a tree.

- Think of parts of your body that branch, such as your arms and your fingers. What else branches? Draw yourself as a tree. Make up a story about your tree.

- Think of many things in nature that branch—lightning, rivers, plants. Draw a picture of one of these.

- *(Pull some weeds and give each child one to study.)* Find the stem, the branches, and the roots. Draw the lines you see, and make them connect like the branches. Talk about other things that branch.

- Draw a forest full of trees. Fill your paper with large and small trees and their leaves. Use your crayons and make the forest green and bright colors. Tell a story about walking in your forest.

✏ Collect leaves of different sizes and shapes. Turn up the underside of a leaf to show its veins. Place a sheet of paper over the leaf, and rub the leaf with the side of a crayon to make a leaf rubbing. This rubbing was done by a pre-kindergarten child. *(You may need to use tape to hold children's leaves in place under their papers.)*

✏ *(Bring small branches to class and distribute them.)* Draw everything you see on the branch. Tell about what you have found.

✏ Your fingers branch like the trunk of a tree. Trace your hand and make your drawing into a fruit tree or another kind of tree that you like. Draw birds and nests in your tree. Pretend you are the mother bird talking to your baby birds. What will you say?

These hand tracings were made into trees. They were done by pre-kindergarten children.

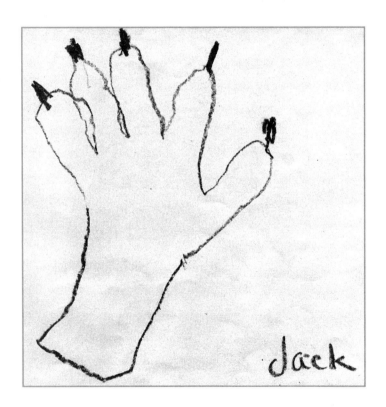

✏ Did you ever pick apples? Draw yourself climbing up an apple tree and picking apples. Do you need a ladder? Tell a story about it.

✏ Draw a tree that you could climb. Draw big branches reaching out. Draw yourself climbing the tree. Make up a story about climbing.

✏ This is a child's drawing of wind blowing through a tree. Draw trees blowing in the wind. Tell about a windy day.

This is a drawing of a tree. Can you count the branches? Do you think this drawing was done in summer? Why or why not? With your finger, follow the trunk of the tree up to each branch.

9. Drawing with Math

- Draw lines across your paper with different colors of crayons. Make each line different. One can be straight. The next one can be wavy. Another can be zigzag. Draw many of the same lines, but use different colors for each line. Fill your paper with interesting lines.

- *(Using a long piece of string or rope, have four children make a square while holding the rope.)* What shape is this? How many sides does it have? Draw three squares and draw something in each one. Ask other children to guess what you have drawn.

- Name things that are square. Draw some of them. Tell about your drawings.

- Find repeated patterns. Look for plaid skirts, fences, and the American flag. Draw your own repeated pattern. Choose one shape or line and draw it many times. Tell about why you chose your shape or line.

- *(Using a long piece of string or rope, have three children make a triangle while holding the rope.)* What shape is this? How many sides does a triangle have? How many children do you need to make one? Draw it on your paper. Draw around it to make it into something you know. Tell about it. Name objects shaped like a triangle.

- List things around you that are round. Draw them. Ask your classmates to guess what each one is.

- Draw a large circle. Now draw two small circles. Draw three circles inside the large circle. Add color to make your drawing exciting.

- Draw a circle. Think of something that has a circle in it. Draw the object from your circle. Tell about your drawing.

- Draw two sets of four apples. Tell about a food that is made with apples.

✏ *(Make a class number book. Distribute 9" × 12" paper folded to 6" × 9."*
Assign each child a number.) Draw your number on one side of the paper.
On the other side, draw the same number of things, such as wheels,
balloons, kites, and so on. *(Arrange the pages in numerical order, and*
attach them on the back with transparent tape to make an accordion-fold
book.)

Give children construction paper triangles about 4" high. Ask them to paste their
triangles wherever they wish on their papers. Have them make their triangles into
something by drawing around and in them. When they have finished, ask them to
tell about their drawings.

✏ How many of you
know what a hot air
balloon looks like?
(Discuss hot air
balloons and the
baskets where people
sit.) Here is a picture
of a big hot air
balloon. Draw a circle
on your paper and
make it into a hot air
balloon. Draw lines
down from it to a
basket where people
sit. Decorate your
balloon with different
colors and a design.
Tell a story about
going up in a hot air
balloon.

10. Cutting Shapes

Eye-hand coordination is an essential skill. Learning how to handle scissors is an important way of developing this skill. Spend time on direct cutting with children.

Using a paper cutter, cut sheets of construction paper along the 9" side to make nine connected strips. Begin at one end and leave 1" uncut as shown in the diagram at the right. Distribute 9" × 12" sheets of colored construction paper. Ask children to hold the paper horizontally and cut the entire sheet into strips that are about 1/2" wide. Allow children to exchange strips so each child has a variety of colors. Distribute the sheets you have prepared. Teach the concept of under/over and over/under in alternating lines. Then, have children begin to weave the 1/2" strips into the full sheet.

*Cut colored construction paper into 6" squares. Ask children to cut a shape out of the middle of their squares. Tell them to keep the outside square shape. Arrange the **positive** and **negative** shapes in a checkerboard pattern on a bulletin board.*

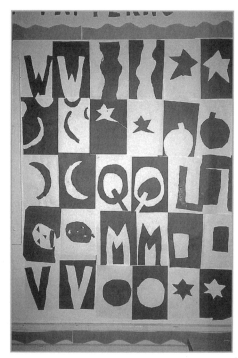

✏ *(Distribute two sheets of 9" × 12" construction paper to each child.)* Fold one piece of construction paper in half. Hold the folded edge with one hand, and cut from the bottom of your paper to the top. Cut in and out. Make a funny line with your scissors. Now open your paper, and look at the shape you made. What could it be? Glue it on your other sheet of paper, and draw on and around the shape to make a funny person or animal.

✏ *(Distribute 6" × 9" sheets of construction paper.)* Cut many strips of paper. Then cut many little squares.

✏ *(Distribute 9" × 12" sheets of construction paper.)* On this sheet of paper, arrange your strips and squares to make little people. The strips will be arms, legs, and bodies. The squares will be heads. Make the little people look like they are dancing. Glue the pieces on your paper when you are ready.

A pre-kindergarten child drew this figure and cut it out. Here is the figure and the cutting. Such precise cutting is unusual at this age, but it can be done with practice.

Draw large letters of the alphabet on sheets of paper and duplicate a set for each child. Ask children to cut along the lines.

11. Drawing Helps Children Learn to Read

Vocabulary development is greatly advanced by drawing objects and labeling them. Drawing also helps children learn a second language. Try some of these exercises as a preparation for reading.

Create a picture dictionary. Name something and have children draw a picture of it on individual sheets of paper. As children are drawing their pictures, help them write the word that describes what they are drawing under their pictures. When children have finished, alphabetize the pages. Continue adding to the dictionary throughout the year.

✏ Draw fruit and vegetables. *(Write the words for each fruit or vegetable that children draw. Say the words and ask children to repeat them.)* Learn to read the names of the fruit and vegetables you drew.

✏ Draw something that starts with the letter *A.* Show your drawing to the class and ask them to guess what it is. *(Do this often with different letters of the alphabet. You might dedicate a week for each letter of the alphabet. Ask children to bring in objects that start with that letter.)*

Create a class alphabet book. Assign a letter to each child. Distribute 8 1/2" × 11" sheets of paper. Show children how to hold their papers horizontally and then fold them in half. Help them find the left side of their papers.

✏ Draw a large letter on the left side of your paper. Decorate your letter with lines and patterns. *(Help children find the right side of their papers.)* On the right side of your paper, draw something that starts with your letter. *(Alphabetize children's papers. Attach papers edge-to-edge with transparent tape. Refold this into an accordion-fold book.)*

Read a story from a library book, and ask children to draw what they hear. Have children tell about their drawings.

12. Drawing Parts of the Body

These lessons are preliminary exercises to prepare for drawing figures. Connect them to science lessons.

- Trace your hand. Draw fingernails on each finger and the thumb. Talk about all the things you can do with your hands.

Show a diagram of the eye and point to each part—pupil, iris, eyelids, eyelashes, tear ducts, and eyebrows.

- Sit opposite a partner and draw his or her eyes as large as you can. Put in every detail. Tell about something wonderful that you see in your partner's eyes. (*A kindergarten child drew this 12" × 18" picture after a science lesson about the parts of the eye.*)

Teach about the parts of the ear—the earlobe, the eardrum, and so on.

- Look at your partner's ear. Draw every line you see in it. Hearing is a wonderful gift. People who cannot hear "listen" with their eyes. (*Teach some simple sign language.*) Try to use these signs to talk.

- Draw your partner's face. Draw a large oval on your paper. Now draw the lines of your partner's hair. See how the front of the hair comes down into the oval of the head. Now draw eyes, ears, nose, and mouth. Draw the lines of the neck starting just below the ears.

Start this exercise in September, and do monthly self-portraits. Keep and date self-portraits so children can see their development at the end of the school year. Have children draw small self-portraits for the cover of their sketchbooks.

- Draw the faces of everyone in your family. Think about details such as eyelashes and eye color. Does anyone wear glasses? Does your father have a mustache or a beard? Tell about each person.

- Take off a shoe, and have another child trace your foot on your paper. Draw your toes and toenails.

13. Drawing People

Drawing people is an important skill that helps children develop perceptual skills. Do not accept stick figures. Use a Halloween skeleton to teach about the structure of the human body. Ask children to stand and feel their own shoulder bones. Move the skeleton's arm to show how the shoulder joint allows the arm to move in all directions. Compare this movement to a joystick. Bend the skeleton's elbow, and point out how different this joint is. Compare it to a door on its hinges. Hold the skeleton's arms close to the body, and bend them at the elbows. Point out that the elbows come to the waist, and the hands reach to the thighs. Show children the hipbones and how the legs attach to them. Bend the backbone and marvel at the ways we are able to move.

Start with an overhead projector or a strong lantern light. Have a child stand in the light and cast a shadow on the wall. Hang mural paper on the wall, and trace the shadow. You can do this for each child. Help children cut out their figures. Then, one at a time have each child lie on a piece of mural paper and trace his or her figure. Help children see the difference between their shadows and their traced figures.

- Draw your face and hair. Draw the bones that are in your body—backbone, ribs, shoulder bone, arm and leg bones. Look at the skeleton and talk about how your body works.

- *(Make another figure for each child and distribute the figures.)* Where your head is, draw the things that are in your head. Where your hands are, draw the things you like to make. Where your feet and legs are, draw the places you like to go. Where your stomach is, draw the foods you like to eat. Where your heart is, draw the people you love. Tell about your drawing.

Gesture Drawing

Gesture drawing of a figure is drawing the outside line of the body shape—no features of the face, no clothes details. Start with the head and follow all the way around the body with your eyes—neck, shoulder, elbow, hand, back to the body, down to the waist, hip, knee, foot, back up the leg, and up the other side to the head. The aim is to see the all-over proportions of the body and the way it moves.

Have a child pose. Have the other children start drawing the figure. Ask them to draw the head at the top of the paper. Then verbally guide children to look at the model, and draw the neck from the head to the shoulder. Next, have them draw across the shoulder to the arm and down the arm to the elbow and then to the wrist. Next have them draw the hand and continue, drawing the underside of the arm, getting back to the body. Have them draw to the waist, to the hip, to the knee, and finally, to the foot. Do this many times, even daily, until all children see the form. Try standing behind the model and tracing the path of the model's line with your finger.

These drawings show many different approaches to the figure. Draw figures many times, each time looking for body parts and connections of arms and legs to shoulders and hips, and so on.

- Play "Statue Maker." When you tell your model to "freeze," draw the pose.

- Draw yourself and your friends at a playground. Think of the slides, swings, and other things you like at the playground.

- Draw your family at dinner. Draw the table and its places. Where does each member of your family sit? Describe your dinner.

- Draw each member of your family. Tell a story about them.

These are a five-year-old child's drawings of her family.

This drawing of me (on the right) is by a four-year-old child. Earrings, the pattern on my dress, and even my yellow car were added. The gesture drawing of me below is by a four-year-old girl who sat next to me on an airplane.

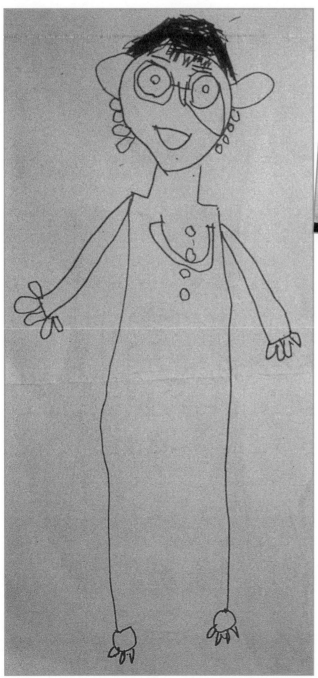

✏ Draw your grandparents. Tell about them. This is a child's drawing of his grandparents.

This drawing of a mother and her child is by American artist Mary Cassatt. Tell a story about the people in the drawing. What is the mother saying to her child? Draw a picture of yourself with your mother or someone who takes care of you.

14. Drawing Animals

Drawing animals, birds, fish, and insects connects directly to your science curriculum. Understanding the structure and body parts of these creatures is important in drawing them. Build up a collection of photographs and make them available to your children to study carefully. Use the Internet and National Geographic *films to observe both the structure and movement of animals. Encourage your children to draw animals in the same way that they draw objects and figures, by letting their eyes direct their hands and using simple flowing lines that express the shape and movement.*

✏ Draw a picture of an animal that you make up. Give it an elephant's trunk or a tiger's stripes—whatever you want. Then tell the class about your animal, where it lives, what it eats, and so on. Give it a name.

✏ Draw your pet or a pet you would like to have. Tell the class about it.

✏ Draw an animal in a forest. Try to let it hide in the trees and grass. The color of animals and their stripes and spots help them to hide. Imagine yourself in a forest, and tell a story about finding an animal hiding there.

✏ *(Distribute safety scissors and 3" × 4" sheets of construction paper.)* Cut many little pieces of paper. Put them together to make an animal. When you have shaped your animal, glue each little piece one at a time. Make up a name for your animal.

This rabbit was made from many little pieces.

Create a class alphabet book of animals. Assign a letter of the alphabet to each child. Then go through the alphabet, eliciting the name of an animal from each child. Fold sheets of 9" × 12" drawing or construction paper in half and distribute one sheet to each child. When children have completed the following exercise, sequence their pages, attach them on the back with tape, and make an accordion-fold book.

✏ *(Help children find the left side of their papers.)* Draw your letter on the left side of your paper. *(Help children find the right side of their papers.)* Draw your animal on the right side.

✏ *(This sculpture of a horse with a man riding on it was created over two thousand years ago by an Etruscan artist. Etruscans lived in Italy.)* Look at the horse's mane. Now look at the man's helmet. Are they alike? What do you think the artist is telling us about his horse? Do you think it ran fast? Draw a horse that you would like to ride. Think of all the parts of a horse—head, neck, mane, body, legs, and tail. Tell about horseback riding.

✏ This is a drawing of a cow by German artist Lovis Corinth. Tell what you know about cows. Where do they live? What do they give us? Draw a cow.

You may want to locate Panama on a world map and tell children about the Cuna women who live on an island near Panama. They make molas—beautiful stitchery pieces with many layers of colored fabric.

✏ This is a **mola** design of a monkey with three little animals around it. Draw a monkey in a tree. Fill in your paper with branches of the tree. Could your monkey be hanging by its tail from a branch? Tell a story about it.

✏ What do you know about rabbits? What kind of ears do they have? This child drew the head of a rabbit with its long ears. Think of an animal that you like and draw it.

This is a photograph of a zebra. Look at all the stripes on its body. Can you draw a zebra?

15. Drawing Birds

Talk about the difference between animals and birds—two legs, wings, and so on.

- ✏ Would you like to fly like a bird? Draw a large bird that you could sit on and fly away with. Draw yourself on it and the things you see below you. Tell about your trip.

- ✏ Draw a bird's nest. Put three baby birds in it. Draw a tree branch under it. Tell about the baby birds.

- ✏ Draw a tree full of birds. Make them beautiful colors. Think about the parts of a bird's body—head, beak, wings, tail, legs, and feet (claws). Make different-colored birds. Make up a story about your birds.

- ✏ Draw a large bird on drawing paper. *(Cut out each bird and make a class tree full of birds. You might make the tree on a bulletin board with yarn, stapling it into the shape of a tree and branches.)*

✏ Draw a stuffed bird.

This is a drawing of a soft stuffed chick by a pre-kindergarten child.

✏️ This is a drawing of a long-legged bird called a sandhill crane. Where do you think it lives? Why does it have long legs and a long beak? What does it eat? *(Elicit from children that the sandhill crane lives in shallow water and uses its beak to catch fish.)* Draw a pond with cranes standing in shallow water. Make up a song about cranes.

Sandhill crane

✏ This sculpture of a bird is by an Eskimo carver. He found a chunk of soapstone and looked at it until he saw the shape of the bird. Then he carved away just enough so that we can find the bird. Look for the bird's head, beak, wings, and feet. Draw two shapes on your paper. Then look at them until you can see birds. Add wings, a tail, or whatever you need to make two birds. Make up a story about your birds.

✏ This is another mola design showing a bird catching a worm for its breakfast. Draw a picture of a bird bringing a worm back to its nest to feed the baby birds. Draw the nest in the branches of a tree. Make your drawing into a mola by using bright colors and lines for stitches. Write a story about the mother bird.

16. Drawing Fish

Use charts, videos, and books to show the parts of a fish—body, eyes, mouth, gills, scales, fins, and tail. Look for many sizes, shapes, and colors of fish. Look for the beautiful patterns on the bodies of tropical fish.

✐ Imagine yourself as a deep sea diver down in the ocean. Draw many of the beautiful fish that swim by you. Use crayons or markers to make beautiful colors and patterns. Give some of your fish long fins like an angelfish. Tell a story about deep sea diving.

This is a five-year-old's drawing of a fish.

✐ Find seashells and draw them. Talk about how shellfish live inside these shells. How do the shellfish move?

✐ Draw wavy lines across your paper, and pretend that it is the ocean. Draw a fish jumping out of the water. Tell about why you think fish jump.

Draw a huge whale. Whales are really mammals, not fish. They need to breathe air. When they want to breathe, they come to the surface of the ocean and spout water. Draw a huge spray of water coming from your whale. Find out about where whales like to live. Do they live in cold water or warm tropical water?

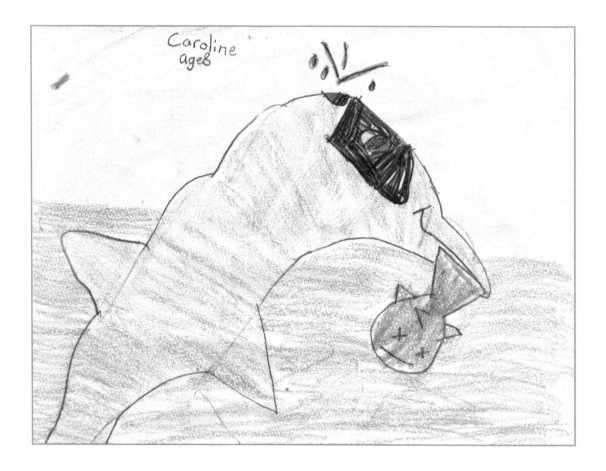

✏ Do you know what a sea horse looks like? This is a fifth-grade child's drawing of a sea horse. Sea horses are very tiny creatures, just a few inches tall. Draw a sea horse. Could you invent a sea rabbit?

17. Drawing Insects

As you teach about insects in science, encourage drawing as a way of making visible the shapes and body parts of insects. Use videos, books, and the Internet to learn about life cycles of the butterfly and other insects.

✏ *(If it is possible to get an "ant farm," children would learn much from watching it.)* Ants live under the ground. They dig tunnels and lay their eggs underground. Draw a line near the top of your paper. This is the ground. Under the line draw tunnels where the ants live. Draw a place where their eggs are stored. Tell about how ants work together.

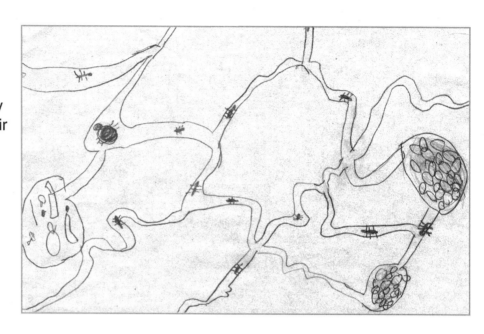

✏ What color is a ladybug? What kind of spots does it have? Can a ladybug fly? Draw a large ladybug on your paper.

This is a child's drawing of a ladybug.

✏ Draw a garden where a ladybug can fly. Tell about how a ladybug decides which flower to land on.

✏ Draw a long worm on your paper. Then draw a bird that is about to eat it. Tell a story about the bird and the worm.

✏ *(This is a **brush drawing** of flying insects. Talk about insects that fly. Count the four wings.)* Fill your paper with a sky full of flying insects. Make them bright colors. Make up a song about them.

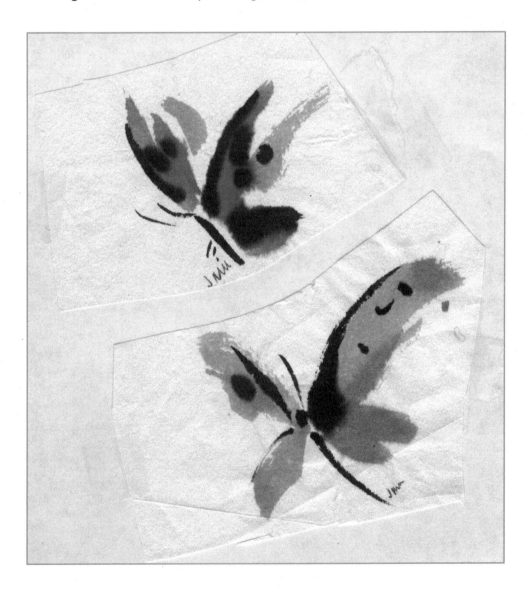

✏ Can you draw a butterfly? Here are two butterflies. The first one is a very large Japanese kite. The one on the next page is a child's drawing. How do butterflies move? Look for the head, the body, and the four wings. See how the wings are the same on both sides. Draw your own butterfly, and draw designs on its wings.

Ellie® Oconnr

How many legs does a spider have? This drawing of a spider in its web was done by a pre-kindergarten child. Draw a spider and draw its web around it. Tell about how spiders catch insects in their webs.

✏ This is a drawing of a dragonfly by a pre-kindergarten child. Why do you think it is called a dragonfly? Draw an insect with wings. Draw a garden under the insect. Draw many flowers for your insect to enjoy.

18. Drawing Buildings

Take a walk to study parts of houses in the neighborhood. Find roofs, chimneys, windows, doors, stairs, porches, and so on. Compare houses to high-rise apartments.

✏ Draw the front of your home or apartment building from memory. Think about doorways, stairs, windows, and roof lines. When you get home, do another drawing while you look at your house. Compare the drawings. Describe your home.

Read aloud or remind children of nursery rhymes and fairy tales such as "The Woman Who Lived in a Shoe" and "Peter Pumpkin Eater."

✏ Draw a house just for yourself. What will it need? How many doors and windows will it have? Where will it be? Will it have trees and flowers outside? Try a different shape. Tell the class about your house.

✏ Draw a house for birds. Can you make it a high-rise for several bird families? This is a picture of one. It was designed and constructed by sculptor Dan Yarborough. Make an invitation to bird families to live in your house.

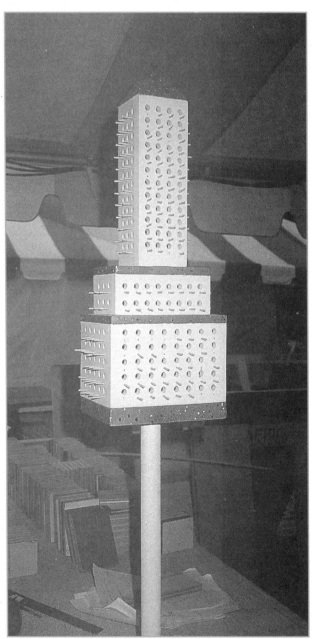

- Draw a row of houses where you and your friends can live next door to each other. Draw all of you outside. Tell a story about your neighborhood.

- *(Read aloud parts of the story,* Alice in Wonderland.*)* Draw the house that Alice was too big for in the story *Alice in Wonderland*. Draw her inside the house. Tell the story of her adventures.

- Draw a playground climbing place. Put in ladders and a slide. Tell about it.

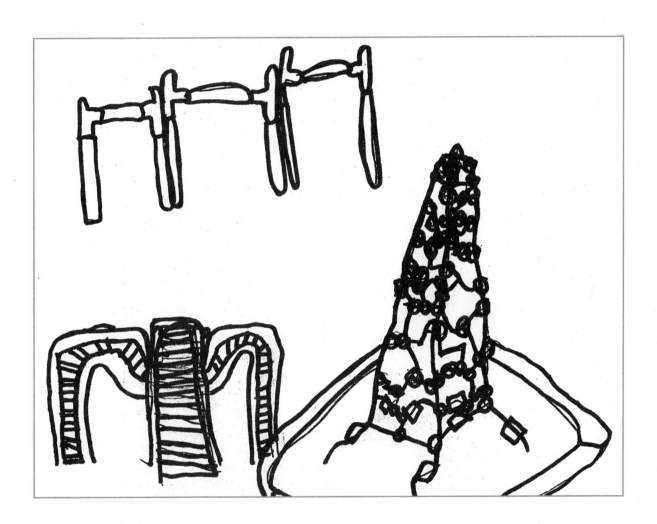

This drawing of a house is by the famous artist Marc Chagall. Look for the door, windows, roof, chimney, fence, and shed in the back. Is one man coming to visit the man standing in the door? Tell a story about the house. Then draw your own house with a chimney, door, roof, windows, and fence. Can you draw a garden in front of your house?

Where can you find a lighthouse? What are lighthouses for? This is a drawing of a lighthouse next to the water. Draw your own lighthouse. Can you draw the water all wavy, like in a storm? Tell about it.

Some houses are on farms. This is a child's drawing of a farm with its barn, silo, and crops. Why do you think the farmer has put a big scarecrow in the field to scare away the birds? Draw a farm. Will there be animals? Tell about it.

This photograph shows a house in Williamsburg, Virginia. Williamsburg was one of the first towns settled by people who came from Europe to live in America. Look for the chimneys on the right and left sides of the house. Find the door stoop—three steps up to the door. Count the windows. Look for the white picket fence. Draw a house with chimneys, windows, and a door. What else will you draw for your house?

✏ Draw your favorite part of a playground. Is it the slide, the swings, or the jungle gym? Draw yourself on your favorite ride. Tell about playing there with your friends.

This is a child's drawing of a merry-go-round.

Look with your students at paintings by American artist Edward Hopper, especially his scenes of houses on hills. A five-year-old child drew this while looking at Hopper's Houses on the Beach. *Ask children to draw what they see in other Hopper paintings.*

19. Drawing from Imagination

Imaginative thinking and expressing are essential to learning. It frees the child's mind to make new connections, see relationships, and invent new ideas. The following activities are designed to stimulate this kind of thinking. Be open to your students' ideas. Encourage fantasizing, exaggerating, and combining forms. If your students have an idea for a "Draw and Tell" exercise, listen to it and use it.

✏ Suppose one day you wake up to find everything the wrong color. Draw what you see and tell about it.

✏ Transform a piece of fruit into a car. Give your car a name.

✏ Draw a fantastic bird. Give it huge wings and claws and at least three colors. Tell a story about it.

✏️ Draw a button on your paper. This button thinks it is a *(pause)* what? Imagine it and draw it. Tell about it.

✏️ Draw yourself with a pumpkin head. How will you be dressed? Tell about a party that you will go to as a pumpkin.

✏ Draw yourself as a clown. Give yourself a silly wig and huge feet. Think of many other things that you can draw to make yourself look funny.

✏ Imagine meeting a butterfly that is bigger than you are. Draw the butterfly and yourself. What will you say to it?

✏ What if you were in a garden with flowers taller than you are? Draw yourself walking in the garden, and draw the huge flowers. Make up a story about what happens to you.

✏ Draw a picture of a dream you had. Was it funny or scary?

✏ Draw a very tall person and a little person next to him or her. What are they saying to each other?

✏ *(Draw a large letter on a sheet of paper and duplicate it for each child. Distribute the sheets of paper.)* Look at this letter. What could it be? Use your imagination and draw it to look like someone or something.

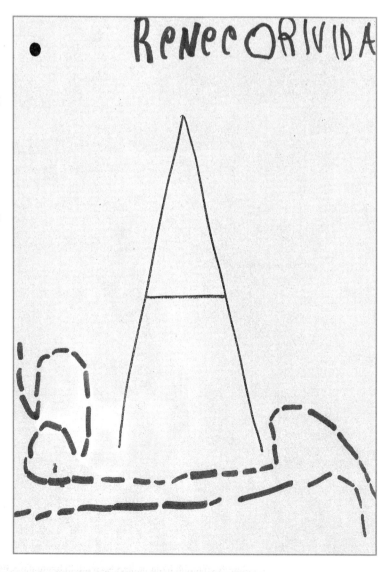

✏ Draw yourself with a big hat. Fill the top of the hat with flowers or fruit.

✏ Bring in some leaves. Glue them to your paper, and draw around them to make them into something else.

✏ The children who drew these pictures read the book *Pete's Bird.* It tells the story of a boy who drew a different kind of bird in school. *(Read the book,* Pete's Bird, *to your children.)* See how many wonderful birds a child's imagination can dream up. Draw one of your own.

20. Encouraging Drawing at Home

Encouraging children to draw at home has many advantages, starting with the possibility of weaning them away from television and computer games. When children develop a habit of drawing they will not only enjoy it, but they will build confidence that will last a lifetime. Give credit for drawings done at home. Take time to look at them and, once in a while, create a display of "home" themes such as my family, kitchen shapes, pets, and so on. You may want to photocopy the following message and lessons and send them home with your students. Encourage them to add to the list ideas they have for drawing.

A Message to Parents

Your child is being encouraged to draw in school. Drawing is a natural skill in every child. Here are some ideas that you can share with your child to help build his or her skills. The lessons are designed to sharpen perception and all of the sensory powers. Nurturing perception in your child is a way of relating to him or her, building confidence in him or her, and having a really good time together.

Never tell your children that their drawings are not good. Ask them to tell you about their drawings. Realize that drawing is just as individual as handwriting, and it will reveal wonderful insights about your children if you listen to them and support them.

Learning is more exciting when it is brought home from school. The following goals and activities will help you continue your child's learning at home.

Goals

1. To relate your child's learning to real life.

2. To provide a learning situation that can enrich the background of both you and your child.

3. To bring the family together in active, creative endeavors.

4. To be aware of and appreciative of your child's progress, efforts, and individual expression.

Try These Activities with Your Child

✏ Take a "shape walk," looking at objects in your home and talking about their shapes—the parts of a chair, the shape of a lamp and its shade, pots and pans in the kitchen, and so on. Listen to your child's words, and teach him or her new words to identify and describe objects.

✏ Take a "color walk," looking for one color everywhere you can find it. Help your child to see variations—light or dark, bright or dull.

✏ Take a "texture walk," looking at and feeling surfaces, and describing them as smooth, fuzzy, soft, hard, shiny, rough, crinkly, and so on. Do rubbings with the side of a crayon on surfaces you find.

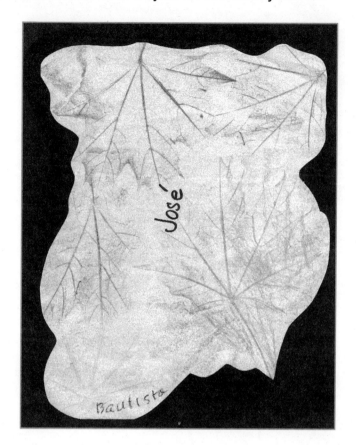

✏ Make an alphabet book of things in your home. Get 26 sheets of paper and draw a letter of the alphabet at the top of each one. As your child finds an object, ask him or her to draw a picture of it on the proper page. You can add to this by finding pictures in magazines and cutting them out. Add more pages as needed.

✏ Encourage your child to collect round objects, square objects, hard or soft things, and so on. Spend time sorting and talking about these objects.

✏ Look for rhythms that are part of your daily life. Everything about us is in constant motion. We move. We breathe. Our hearts beat. Stop and listen. Listen to wind blowing, to leaves rustling, and to water boiling. With your child, beat out the rhythm of a truck going by, the tick of a clock, and the pattern of music.

✏ Look out a window with your child and observe all the movements you can see.

✏ Look for repeated patterns with your child. Sometimes, even things that we know stand still seem to move because they make our eyes move. For example, a picket fence, stacks of cans or boxes in a supermarket, stripes on a dress, and so on. Ask your child to draw these patterns.

✏ Find all the repeated lines and shapes you can. Notice patterns that repeated lines make—some form rows, others make circles (such as spokes of a bicycle wheel). The needles of pine trees all shoot out from a stem. Some, like pine needles on the ground, form a busy pattern of overlapping diagonals.

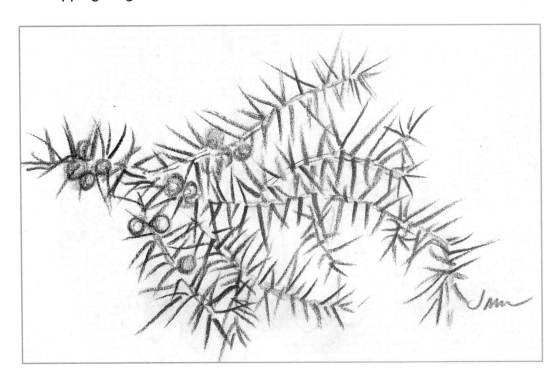

✏ Listen to music together. Tap the beat of the music, march to it, or dance to it.

Drawing at Home

✏ Cut strips of paper and play pattern games. Take turns building a repeated pattern (lines in a row) or an opposing pattern (criss-cross). (This relates to math concepts in school.)

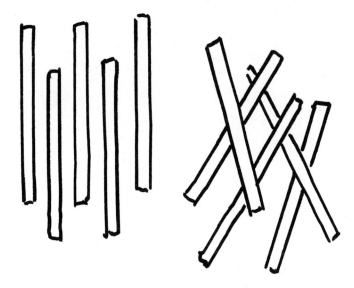

✏ Watch educational television programs together. Draw animals or flowers or other images from the program. Talk together about the places and things you see.

✏ Draw pieces of fruit and vegetables. Draw a banana. Then, peel it halfway, and draw it again. After you eat the banana, draw the peel.

✏ Use a large brown bag to make a costume. Cut holes for head and arms and draw the costume together.

✏ Draw toys.

✏ Draw pets.

✏ Draw your child's room. Look for all the details.

✏ Draw flowers in your garden or potted plants in your home.

✏ Look at trees together. Use a finger and, with one eye closed, follow the trunk of the tree up to the branch and out each branch. Draw the tree.

✏ Encourage ideas from your child for things to draw.

Glossary

balance - a state of stability or equilibrium. In art it can be symmetrical or asymmetrical, achieved with color, shape, line, and proportion.

bilateral symmetry - same on both sides of a central axis

branching - dividing from the stem

brush drawing - drawing done with a paint brush rather than a pencil or drawing tool

composition - the organization of parts to make a unified whole

eye parts - pupil, iris, eyelids, eyelashes, tear ducts, and eyebrows

flower parts - petals, sepal, stamen, stem, and leaves

gesture drawing - a quick line recording of the outer edge of a figure

line - curved, diagonal, horizontal, flowing, straight, wavy, wiggly, and zigzag

mola - a brightly colored applique fabric design sewn by hand by Cuna Indian women in the San Blas Islands off the coast of Panama

mosaic - a design composed of many small pieces

perceptual - pertaining to the senses, particularly sight

positive/negative - figure and background, solid and open

proportion - the relation of parts to the whole in a composition

radial symmetry - going from the center outward

repeat pattern - design made from repeating a line or shape

rhythm - patterned repeat of an element (color, line, shape, and so on) in art

shape - a flat area enclosed by its boundary

space - the designed surface of a picture; the illusion of depth in a 2-D plane

symmetry - sameness

texture - the visual (simulated) and/or tactile (actual) quality of a surface

Name _____

School Months

	1	2	3	4	5	6	7	8	9
uses details									
carefully colors shapes									
completes drawings									
cuts neatly									
glues neatly									
shows craftsmanship									
uses descriptions									

Additional Comments:

_____

_____

_____

_____

_____